IMAGES
of America

BALTIMORE
CLOSE UP

The May Flower Mart is a favorite Baltimore event held in Mount Vernon around the Washington Monument, the nation's first major memorial to honor George Washington, completed in 1829. This is a view of a Flower Mart in the 1960s. (Courtesy of the Star-Spangled Banner Flag House.)

IMAGES
of America

BALTIMORE
CLOSE UP

Christopher T. George

ARCADIA

Published by Arcadia Publishing,
an imprint of Tempus Publishing, Inc.
2 Cumberland Street
Charleston, SC 29401

Printed in Great Britain.

Library of Congress Catalog Card Number: 98-86387

For all general information contact Arcadia Publishing at:
Telephone 843-853-2070
Fax 843-853-0044
E-Mail arcadia@charleston.net

For customer service and orders:
Toll-Free 1-888-313-BOOK

Visit us on the internet at http://www.arcadiaimages.com

To my darling wife, Donna, as ever, for her patience and support.

CONTENTS

ABOUT THE PHOTOGRAPHS

Most of the older photographs in this book came from the collections of Ross J. Kelbaugh and Ann Naito Haney. In addition to photographs of the people of Baltimore, both collectors lent me views of the city taken by local photographers. These included stereo views by W. M. Chase, whose series, "Metropolitan and Suburban Scenery, Baltimore, Md.," affords a valuable record of the city in the 1870s. Mr. Kelbaugh also provided prints made from Chase's glass negatives. Photography Collections at the University of Maryland Baltimore County provided many of the Hughes Company images that appear here. The James F. Hughes Company was a firm of commercial photographers that worked in Baltimore from the later decades of the 19th century through the Second World War. The Hughes images offer a rare and valuable look at different aspects of the city, from buildings and public occasions to private family moments. Several of the pictures of harbor workers and of Baltimore harbor itself in the early years of the 20th century came from the National Archives and the Maryland State Archives. Photographs of the Flag House over the years and other images were kindly provided by the Star-Spangled Banner Flag House. Photographs from the 1930s, World War II, and postwar years were provided by Brenda Weber of Mamie's Café, Hampden, and her father, Ben Weber, and also by Dottie Linthicum. Pictures of the Duke and Duchess of Windsor taken by Emma M. Lintner were lent by her granddaughter, Sandy Stinebaugh. The photograph of Babe Ruth by Leroy Merriken of *The Baltimore Sun* was supplied by Dan Rodricks. In addition to the above-named persons, my thanks go to Tom Beck, John Beck, Jerry Schnitzer, Beth Miller, Geoffrey M. Footner, John M. Hyson Jr., Elise DiPaula Erlandson, Kathy Lee Erlandson Liston, and Norman Greenspun. I also thank my mother, Yoria C. George, for lending family pictures from our early years in Baltimore City.

INTRODUCTION

Baltimore, one of the great cities of the United States, makes an ideal subject for a photographic history. When the photographic age dawned in the 1840s with the first dageurrotypists opening businesses in the city, Baltimore was a booming industrial seaport. The hundreds of photographers who worked in the city over the coming decades would have much to record. These talented artists who documented the life of the city and its people made it a relatively easy job to assemble this collection, which provides a celebration of Baltimore and its people over the last century and a half.

The city was incorporated in 1797 in the midst of a surge in growth that saw the community expand from the small town it had been during the American Revolution to being the nation's third largest city at the time of the War of 1812, behind New York and Philadelphia. It was in September 1814 during the latter war that the British attempted to sack and burn Baltimore just as they had sacked and burned the nation's capital, Washington, D.C., three weeks earlier. The bombardment of Fort McHenry at the mouth of Baltimore harbor led Georgetown lawyer Francis Scott Key, aboard a truce ship to negotiate the release of Upper Marlboro physician Dr. William Beanes, to write "The Star-Spangled Banner" in celebration of the fact that the famed fifteen-star flag was still flying over the Star Fort.

Thus Baltimore already had much to celebrate when the age of photography dawned. As photographic processes changed and improved, photography became the vogue and many of the citizens had themselves recorded by the camera lens, as we will see vividly shown in these pages. Moreover, a remarkable number of photographers and photographic companies recorded the city, its monuments, and its people at work and play.

This book focuses as much on the people of Baltimore as the streets and buildings that have been the feature of previous photographic histories of the city. A city is more than bricks and mortar, and the people of Baltimore have demonstrated for decades that they have heart and resilience. Here we will look at the high and the low, the rich and famous, the poor and downtrodden, the good times and the bad. In short, this picture collection provides a unique look at this exceptional U.S. city.

Although I was not born in Baltimore, I have nevertheless lived in the Baltimore area for the majority of my life. As several pictures here document, my parents and I first came to the city in 1955. I was six years old at the time, and my family were new immigrants from Liverpool, England. Interestingly, as architectural historian Phoebe Stanton once remarked to me, Baltimore has been called "The Liverpool of the East Coast of America." There are a lot of similarities. Both are seaports with large, multi-ethnic working class populations. Baltimore has its brick row houses, Liverpool its terraced houses— same animal, different name. It is thus perhaps not surprising that I am as fond of my adopted city as I am of my birth city. I hope some of my love of Baltimore shows through in these pages.

One
STAR-SPANGLED
BANNER CITY

The city streets were hung with bunting during the 1914 centennial of the writing of the "Star-Spangled Banner." The Masonic Arch was one of a number of arches set up in celebration of the anniversary. (This photograph and others in this section, are courtesy of the Star-Spangled Banner Flag House Association, Inc.)

Artist R. McGill Mackall painted this oil painting of the making of the original Star-Spangled Banner for the local headquarters of the National Brewing Company. Mary Pickersgill (second from right) is seen sewing the huge 30-by-42-foot 15-star flag with daughter Caroline, as niece Eliza Young holds a candle. The flagmaker received the commission from Major George Armistead, commander of Fort McHenry, who is seen second from left talking to Mary's brother-in-law, Commodore Joshua Barney, as General John Stricker looks on.

Francis Scott Key wrote the poem which forms the words for our national anthem when he realized that the Star-Spangled Banner continued to wave over Fort McHenry despite the 24-hour British bombardment of September 13–14, 1814. This portrait of Key by an unknown artist is thought to have been painted while the poet was a student at St. John's College, Annapolis.

In 1927, the Star-Spangled Banner was suspended at the corner of Park Avenue and Lexington Street to raise funds to help restore the Flag House.

The Key Monument in Eutaw Place in Bolton Hill was a 1910 gift to the city of Baltimore from Charles and Theodore Marburg. The bronze memorial by French sculptor Jean Marius Mercie shows Key with his right hand raised offering up to Columbia his poem, originally titled "Defence of Fort McHenry."

Mrs. Reuben Ross Holloway, president of the Maryland Society of the United States Daughters of 1812, championed the movement to make "The Star-Spangled Banner" our national anthem. On April 15, 1929, local Congressman J. Charles Linthicum introduced the bill to make it our country's anthem during the 71st U.S. Congress. The bill passed a year later, and on March 3, 1931, President Herbert Hoover signed it into law.

The Old Defenders who fought to save the city in 1814 at North Point and Fort McHenry gathered in 1880 for this portrait taken in Druid Hill Park at the time of the sesquicentennial of Baltimore Town. They are, from left to right, Samuel Jennings, Asbury Jarrett, George Bass, James Morford, William Batchellor (holding the flagpole), James McCoy, William Stites, Henry Lightner, Darius Wheeler, Elijah Stansbury, Nathan Watts, and Edward Danaker.

The 1793 home of Mary Pickersgill, maker of the Star-Spangled Banner, is located at Pratt and Albemarle Streets, east of the Inner Harbor. In this view, taken around 1907, neighborhood children in knickerbockers play in the cobbled street. Adjoining the Flag House at left is a barber who advertises shaves for 5¢!

14

On June 14, 1927 (Flag Day), the City of Baltimore formally turned the Flag House over to the Star-Spangled Flag House Association. Here the first curator, Mr. Arthur P. Sewall, a blind World War I veteran, stands in front of the restored house. The store next door appears to have changed hands since the last photograph was taken, although it remains a barber's. The adjoining buildings have since been demolished.

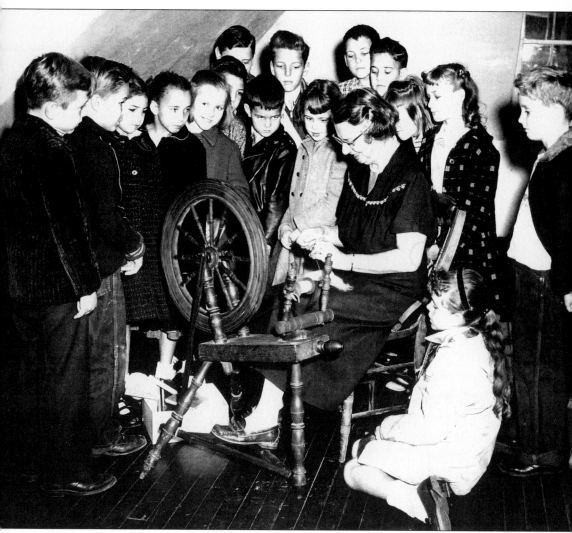

The Star-Spangled Banner Flag House offers an ongoing series of programs. In this photograph taken around 1963, Mrs. Weiss demonstrates for a group of curious schoolchildren how to use a period spinning wheel.

Two
FAMOUS IN BALTIMORE

In 1803, merchant's daughter Elizabeth Patterson (left) married French ruler Napoleon Bonaparte's younger brother Jerome (right) in a celebrated society wedding. Two years later, she gave birth to a son, Jerome Napoleon Bonaparte. But Emperor Napoleon had the marriage annulled. He created Jerome King of Westphalia and made him marry a German princess. Betsy Bonaparte never remarried.

Her mother ran a boarding house on Biddle Street, but twice-divorced Baltimore socialite Wallis Warfield Simpson rocked the British Empire in the 1930s through her liaison with Edward, Prince of Wales, heir to the throne. Rather than give up the woman he loved, Edward abdicated the throne. The couple lived in exile in France and the Bahamas as the Duke and Duchess of Windsor.

Here the Duke and Duchess are seen in Hunt Valley while on a visit to Maryland in April 1959. The Duchess was wearing a pink outfit. She graciously removed her sunglasses to permit these private photographs to be taken by Emma M. Lintner. (Both photographs courtesy of Sandy Stinebaugh.)

Babe Ruth found fame with the New York Yankees after a brief spell with the Baltimore Orioles. Here he is in May 1930, playing in an exhibition game between the Yankees and Orioles at the old Oriole Park, 29th Street and Greenmount Avenue. A statue was recently unveiled at Oriole Park at Camden Yards to honor the hometown boy whose father once ran a tavern on the site of the present-day ballpark. (Photo by Leroy Merriken, *The Baltimore Sun*.)

Frederick Douglass was a slave in Fells Point, Baltimore, before escaping to the north on a train from President Street Station in 1838. (Collection of Ross J. Kelbaugh.)

This statue of Douglass by James E. Lewis in front of Holmes Hall on the campus of Morgan State University was dedicated on October 20, 1956, at a time when segregation still existed in the city.

Barnum's City Hotel stood where the Clarence Mitchell Jr. Courthouse now stands at Calvert and Fayette Streets. One of the Barnum's most famous guests was Charles Dickens. The British writer, infamous for his criticism of Americans, praised Barnum's Hotel for "having enough water to wash himself." (Collection of Ross J. Kelbaugh.)

Writer Edgar Allan Poe was born in Boston in 1809 to David and Elizabeth Poe, itinerant actors. From 1829 to 1835, he lived in Baltimore with his aunt, Maria Clemm, and his cousin Virginia, who became his wife. This rare, now lost, daguerreotype of Poe at around 32 shows him as a city childhood sweetheart later remembered him—mustacheless. The picture was published in *The Critic*, April 1905.

In October 1849, on a visit to the city, Poe died in mysterious circumstances after being found unconscious outside an East Lombard Street tavern. This imposing marble tomb was erected in the Westminster graveyard at Greene and Fayette Streets in 1875 with money raised in a campaign of pennies raised by city schoolchildren. (Photography Collections, University of Maryland Baltimore County.)

The Shot Tower at Front and Fayette Streets is a well-known city landmark. Built in 1828, it was at that time reputed to be the tallest structure in the nation at 234 feet. It manufactured lead shot for duck hunters around the Chesapeake Bay—molten lead was dropped through perforated pans into a tank of cold water. Legend maintains that on April Fool's Day, 1831, Poe staged a hoax that drew a crowd to see a man fly from the top of the tower to Lazaretto Light near Fort McHenry, 2.5 miles away. (Collection of Ross J. Kelbaugh.)

Charles Carroll of Carrollton, the last surviving signer of the Declaration of Independence, lived long enough to lay the first stone of the B&O Railroad in 1828, at the age of 91 years.

"Cleopatra's Needle," in the shape of a wood-and-plaster replica of the famous Egyptian obelisk, was one of the sights citizens enjoyed during the 1880 sesquicentennial of the founding of Baltimore Town. It stood at the intersection of Lombard, Howard, and Liberty Streets.

Henry Louis (H. L.) Mencken was a tough *Baltimore Sun* newspaperman and social critic. He commented with acerbic wit on such sensations of the day as the Scopes "Monkey" Trial. Of German immigrant parentage, he lived until his death in 1956 on Hollins Street in west Baltimore. (Photography Collections, University of Maryland Baltimore County.)

Baltimore-born Cab Calloway was one of a number of African American entertainers from a city that can also boast that it raised the great Billie Holiday and Eubie Blake. Here Cab is seen with his band in a photograph probably taken in the 1940s. (Collection of Ross J. Kelbaugh.)

Three

IN THE STREETS OF BALTIMORE

In this hitherto unpublished view taken around 1858, a well-dressed black man is seen standing at the corner of Monument and Cathedral Streets. Note the Basilica of the Assumption visible in the center distance. (Collection of Ross J. Kelbaugh.)

On February 7, 1904, the center of Baltimore was hit by a fire that rendered whole city blocks into rubble. (Courtesy of Norman Greenspun.)

The great swathe of destruction in downtown Baltimore luckily spared City Hall, built in 1876, seen at top right in this view.

Militiamen on guard duty in the aftermath of the fire share a hot drink and a joke.

The fire finally stopped at Market Place west of the Jones Falls, by the Power Plant—home today of the Hard Rock Café. (Collection of Ann Naito Haney.)

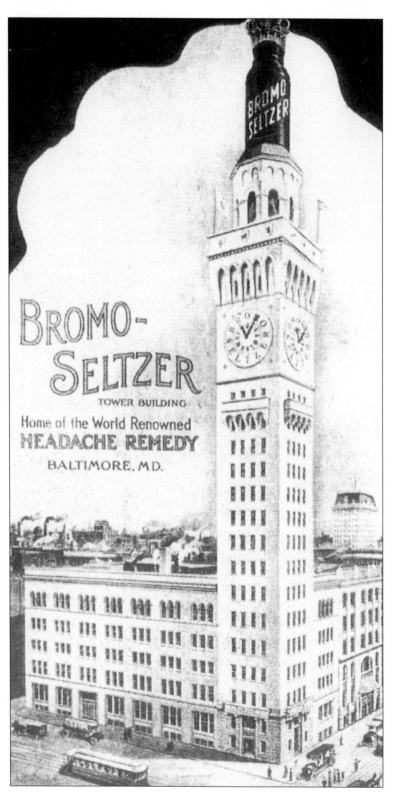

BROMO-
SELTZER
TOWER BUILDING
Home of the World Renowned
HEADACHE REMEDY
BALTIMORE, MD.

The Emerson Drug Company built the Bromo-Seltzer Tower at Lombard and Eutaw Streets in 1911 in the style of the tower of the Palazzo Vecchio in Florence, Italy. It featured on top a giant revolving Bromo-Seltzer bottle which was illuminated at night. The tower did not impress H. L. Mencken. The Sage of Baltimore wrote a typically pithy put-down: "All Baltimoreans may be divided into two classes—those who think the Emerson Tower is beautiful, and those who know better."

The Eutaw House at Eutaw and Baltimore Streets was another of the city's best hotels. In the 1890s, rooms were offered on the American plan "from two dollars and a half to five dollars a day."

In the machinists' strike of 1913, workers striking for an eight-hour day taunted nonstrikers with the label of "scab" still used to this day. (Collection of Ross J. Kelbaugh.)

Ask any Baltimorean: it gets mighty hot and humid in the city in summertime! In the old days, the City used to cool off kids under outdoor showers. These city tykes take great delight in the treat. Nowadays the kids just open the fire hydrants themselves. (Photography Collections, University of Maryland Baltimore County.)

Baltimore's famous Lexington Market was built on land given to the city by Revolutionary War hero John Eager Howard. Although this view by W. M. Chase was taken in the 1870s, it evokes how the market must have appeared in earlier decades of the 19th century. (Collection of Ross J. Kelbaugh.)

Belair Market on Gay Street in Old Town was another of the city's many markets. Here we see the bustling market in a postcard view of the early 1920s. (Collection of Ann Naito Haney.)

Guns for $4.98 are offered from a wagon at Howard Street and Baltimore Streets in this late-19th-century silver print. A sign on the side boasts: "Little Joe's Little Prices" for "Bicycles, Guns, and Sporting Goods." (Collection of Ross J. Kelbaugh.)

The Baltimore Steam Fire Department is shown here, *c.* 1870. (Collection of Ross J. Kelbaugh.)

A group of old-time city firemen proudly pose for the camera with their medals and colors.

The Mount Vernon area exudes elegance. It is no wonder Hollywood production companies shoot scenes there. In a recent film version of Henry James's *Washington Square*, the area around the Washington Monument substituted for Paris. The car speeding down the left side of the street reminds us that the traffic was then two way; closer to our own day, North Charles Street was made one way going north. (Photography Collections, University of Maryland Baltimore County.)

In the top photo, we see the Saratoga Hotel at Saratoga and Howard in 1899. Walk through the swinging doors for a brew and a plate of oysters on the half shell. The bottom photo is either part or all fake. It was not taken on the street but in "Bud's Electric Studio." Our "automobilist" appears proud of his vehicle, but is the car a photographer's prop? (Collection of Ross J. Kelbaugh.)

Mass transit *c.* 1920—Fremont Avenue streetcar no. 30 stops to let off a man on Charles Street who appears to be hurrying off to an appointment. (Photography Collections, University of Maryland Baltimore County.)

The Hillen Tire Co. near Fallsway on Hillen Road is decked out with Star-Spangled Banners and signs advertising "Lee's Tires of Conshohocken" in this view from the 1920s. (Courtesy of Jerry Schnitzer.)

G. H. Martin & Company at 2300 N. Monroe Street offered for sale such top line automobiles as the Packard, Willys Knight, Whippet, and Hupmobile—the latter of which is advertised on the sign at extreme right.

While Hillen Tire contended that their choice brand of Lee's tires "are better," their competitors, the Goodrich Garage, proudly offered "Goodrich Silvertowns." (Collection of Ross J. Kelbaugh.)

Hochschild Kohn's was a chic Howard Street department store. In this Hughes Company photograph, we see a window display for the store's 25th anniversary in November 1922. (Photography Collections, University of Maryland Baltimore County.)

An itinerant photographer with a pony photographed young Ben Weber outside his Highlandtown home on South Curley Street in this snapshot taken in the 1940s. To the right is one of Baltimore's famed marble steps.

The Battle Monument at Calvert and Fayette Streets was designed by French emigré Maximilian Godefroy in 1815 to honor the 41 men who died defending the city in the Battle of Baltimore of 1814. We believe it to be the first true war memorial in the United States. Older readers may remember the newsstand that stood south of the monument. You can just glimpse the roof of Abe Sherman's newsstand at lower right. (Courtesy of the Star-Spangled Banner Flag House.)

Left: The aftermath of a snow storm on Liberty Heights Avenue in West Baltimore in the mid-1950s. Bottom: This elderly gentleman looks relaxed next to his Cadillac. (Courtesy of Yoria C. George and Dottie Linthicum, respectively.)

Four

A City at Play

A "dummy" locomotive pulled a string of cars through Druid Hill Park for the enjoyment of citizens in the 1870s. Here it is seen at the park's Council Grove Station in one of W. M. Chase's stereo views of the 700-acre park. Chase described the park as "remarkable for beauty of landscape and its stately forest trees." (Collection of Ann Naito Haney.)

Couples enjoy a spell on the park's boating lake in a *c.* 1880 photograph by Bacharach (top), while the palmhouse provided another attraction (bottom), as depicted in a picture postcard from the first decade of the 20th century.

A band of young musicians are gathered ready for rehearsal at the park's Moorish bandstand. (Collection of Ross J. Kelbaugh.)

These peak shots of "skinnydippers" of one century ago were termed by photographer W. M. Chase "Free Baths on the Patapsco." (Collection of Ross J. Kelbaugh.)

In contrast to the last guys, these fellows on the Jones Falls at the Old Belvedere Bridge near Greenmount Cemetery elected to keep their clothes on! The bridge carried Guilford Avenue over the Jones Falls.

In the later 19th century, Fort McHenry became a great tourist attraction. The top view shows the 15-inch Rodman cannons that were mounted at the fort after the Civil War as the latest in coastal defense. In the bottom view, ladies with parasols tour the fort near the sally port.

A speed cyclist was captured in 1897 at David J. Wilkes' studio at 213 E. Baltimore Street. Probably the photographer opaqued the negative to remove evidence of the contraption that kept the cyclist upright and that gave the illusion of speed. (Collection of Ross J. Kelbaugh.)

Ethnic dancers with tambourines (top) and
a circus sideshow performer (bottom) were
among the people photographed by city
photographers in the late 19th century.

Two young girls play with their dolls in these studio portraits. (Photographs on these two pages, collection of Ross J. Kelbaugh.)

The old clubhouse at Pimlico Race Course (top) was an ornate fantasy of "Steamboat Gothic" from its construction in 1873 to its final demise in a fire in 1966. Here "Old Hilltop" is seen in a view from the 1890s. Still to be seen today is the Patterson Park pagoda (bottom). Note the two old-time policemen standing at the entrance in this period photo.

Studio photographers often tried to simulate a rustic locale for their customers. Here this bicyclist photographed at the Bachrach studio looks as if he could have been out enjoying the outdoors in Druid Hill Park. (Collection of Ross J. Kelbaugh.)

At top we see the WBAL Radio musicians of 1939 led by Polis Komianis (with baton, center right). These same musicians played at the Park Plaza and other venues. Below, on a more serious note, is a view of the Baltimore Symphony Orchestra at roughly the same period. (Both pictures courtesy of Dottie Linthicum.)

This pre-game warm-up took place before a baseball game at Memorial Stadium, 1955.

Street kids pose for the photographer at a Charles Village adventure playground.

Five

CELEBRATIONS

A parochial school class of 1929 is pictured in this portrait taken at the Reissert Studio on North Gay Street. All of the students have carnations. One girl even has carnations in her hair.

This arch, one of ten erected for the 1880 sesquicentennial of Baltimore Town, stood on Sharp Street at the corner of Redwood. Here we see an excellent example of a stereo view in W. M. Chase's popular "American Views" series. Note the shadowy figures in the street who moved during the 10 to 15 seconds needed to expose the photographic plate. (Collection of Ross J. Kelbaugh.)

This display honoring George Washington was shown during Baltimore's sesquicentennial. Note the arms of Lord Baltimore and the Maryland state motto, which today would not be entirely politically correct, *Fatti Maschii, Parole Femine*—"Manly Deeds, Womanly Words." (Collection of Ross J. Kelbaugh.)

Even at night, the Washington Monument dominates Charles Street, providing a permanent celebration of the life of our first president.

The Yellow Cab Company Christmas Party, December 27, 1922, was photographed by the Hughes Company. (Photography Collections, University of Maryland Baltimore County.)

This African American bride and groom were photographed on January 12, 1939, at the Penn Studio at 903 Pennsylvania Avenue. Note the groom's patent leather shoes. (Collection of Ross J. Kelbaugh.)

A wedding party of the 1940s was photographed at Kinling's Studio at Broadway and Eastern Avenue in Fells Point.

Six

CIVIL WAR BALTIMORE

The first blood of the Civil War was shed in Baltimore on April 19, 1861, when Union troops on their way to Washington, D.C., were attacked by a pro-Southern mob while marching between the President Street and Camden Street train stations. The casualties comprised soldiers and civilians alike and totaled four people dead and three dozen wounded.

This famous cover from *Harper's Weekly* of May 7, 1861, "A Female Rebel in Baltimore," vividly exemplifies Northern belief that the city was a hotbed of Southern sentiment. A young belle flaunts a dress with the Confederate stars and bars while Union troops look on. The base of the Battle Monument can be seen in the background. (Collection of Ann Naito Haney.)

Although the illustration of the young Southern lady parading in Confederate colors might have been an artist's fantasy, the Union crackdown on the city following the April 1861 riot was a grim reality. In July, William Weaver, a local photographer who sometimes worked on commission for *Harper's Weekly*, took this shot of federal troops camped round the Battle Monument. Weaver's photograph, which was used to make a wood engraving that appeared in the magazine, is the only known photograph of soldiers in the streets of Baltimore during the Civil War. (Collection of Ross J. Kelbaugh.)

Fort McHenry, seen in this Civil War illustration by Sachse and Company, became a barracks for the Union army, as well as a prison to house citizens suspected of Southern sympathies. Ironically, one of those arrested was Frank Key Howard, grandson of Francis Scott Key, writer of the "Star-Spangled Banner." (Collection of the author.)

On June 23, 1861, Major General Nathaniel
P. Banks (top) took command in Baltimore,
and he enforced the continuing federal grip
on the city. A year later, Major General John
E. Wool (bottom) took command. Wool, the
oldest general officer in either the Union or
Confederate army, ordered a fresh series of
arrests of citizens thought to be disloyal to the
federal government. (Both photographs from
the collection of Ross J. Kelbaugh.)

Union troops on Federal Hill trained their cannons on the city center for the duration of the war. Baltimore remained an occupied city for the rest of the conflict. The federal government could not allow Baltimore, a mere 50 miles from the nation's capital, to remain pro-Southern. (Collection of the author.)

A carte de visite shows Confederate soldier Charles Johnson, who served in the Second Maryland Artillery, C.S.A. It was taken in 1862 after his discharge due to illness. (Collection of Ross J. Kelbaugh.)

This serious young man appears to bear the problems of the world on his shoulders, possibly because when he was photographed in spring 1864 the Civil War still raged, and would do so for another full year. (Collection of Ann Naito Haney.)

71

The Civil War–era lady at top was photographed in her long flowing gown at the studio of Austrian immigrant J. H. Walzl at 213 Baltimore Street. The lady at bottom, who posed at the Bendann Gallery, appears to be in a more somber mood. Possibly she may be the widow or mother of a soldier killed in the conflict—although admittedly she does not wear black. The bravery of the Confederate women of Maryland was later commemorated with a statue on North Charles Street. We do not know if these two ladies favored the Northern or Southern cause. (Both views from the collection of Ann Naito Haney.)

An African American sailor of the Union
navy is depicted in the top carte de visit.
Photographs of African American
servicemen of the Civil War are rare. The
bottom portrait shows Ezra Hunt, a Union
surgeon. (Both photographs from the
collection of Ross J. Kelbaugh.)

Civil War soldiers were often photographed holding weapons. This Union soldier appears to be holding an officer's sword.

Tragedian John Wilkes Booth, born in Bel Air, Harford County, was outspokenly pro-South, and he may also have acted as a Confederate spy. On the night of April 14, 1865, at Ford's Theater, Washington, D.C., he shot President Abraham Lincoln. After being slain by a Union officer's bullet, the assassin was buried in an unmarked grave in the Booth family plot in Green Mount Cemetery. Copies of this photograph were sold after the assassination by city photographers for 25¢ each. (Both photographs from the collection of Ross J. Kelbaugh.)

Seven

BALTIMORE IN TWO WORLD WARS

A hugely successful World War II masonic dinner to aid the War Bond drive was held on November 8, 1944, at the Alcazar on Cathedral Street, as seen in this Hughes Company photograph. (Courtesy of Jerry Schnitzer.)

These two photographs show two soldiers of the First World War—one real and one play-acting. In the top view, Pvt. Walter A. Williams had his picture taken at Camp Meade on August 31, 1918. He sent it as a picture postcard to Alice Hollis at 1132 Poplar Street. In the bottom view, a young boy dresses up as a soldier, perhaps in imitation of his father. (Both photographs from the collection of Ross J. Kelbaugh.)

The 313th Infantry "Baltimore's Own" march in review up Charles Street in celebration of the end of World War I. Note the base of the Washington Monument visible at right.

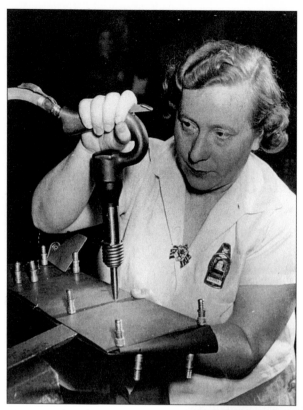

One of the major World War II factories in which Baltimoreans worked was Eastern Aircraft on Broening Highway. Here Mamie and Ben Weber lend a hand in making the Gruman aircraft that would help win the war for the Allies. (Courtesy of Brenda Weber and Mamie's Café, Hampden.)

The *Patrick Henry* (top) was the first of the Liberty Ships built at the Bethlehem-Fairfield shipyards. The *John W. Brown* (bottom) was the 62nd Liberty Ship launched at the yard. The *John W. Brown* remains to this day a floating ambassador and reminder of the bravery and sacrifices of the sailors who ferried war supplies to Europe across the hostile waters of the North Atlantic.

This wartime volunteer ambulance crew was manned by riveters who made Gruman Hellcats and Torpedoes at Eastern Aircraft.

Another photo of workers at Eastern Aircraft reminds us that although the city was still segregated, blacks and whites worked side by side to aid the war effort. (Photos on these two pages courtesy of Ben Weber.)

Taking time out from the worries of World War II, Ben and Mamie Weber and sons Ben Jr. and Edward Weber relax on the front steps of their South Ponca Street home. (Courtesy of Brenda Weber and Mamie's Café, Hampden.)

Eight

BALTIMOREANS AT WORK

Workers at R. E. Roberts & Co. load "Maryland Beauty" oysters on a wagon for shipment out by rail in 1905. (Courtesy of the Maryland State Archives, Special Collections, Robert G. Merrick Archives of Maryland Historical Photographs, SC 1477–4461.)

This young black man photographed around the time of the Civil War worked as a house servant for a Baltimore family. Here he is shown holding his charge, a young white girl.

A Baltimore city policeman of the 1870s. (Photographs on these two pages from the collection of Ross J. Kelbaugh.)

The workers at the Gibbs Preserving Company's Oyster Packery on Boston Street in Canton posed for a photograph in the 1890s. Note that there are several women workers at the left center. Although the oyster-packing industry was seasonal, it provided important opportunities for work for women.

This North Avenue grocery store was photographed *c.* 1900. (Collection of Ross J. Kelbaugh.)

These two ads promote very different commodities: a popular local beer and "Wonder Worker Washing Soap."

WONDER WORKER WASHING SOAP

A Marvel of Inventive Genius.

Washes without rubbing or boiling

Saves time, money and labor, and

Preserves the Clothes.

☞ **SOMETHING OF INTEREST TO EVERYBODY.** ☜

Thousands upon thousands in Baltimore testify
to its wonderful merits.

SHALL IT BRIGHTEN YOUR LIFE AS IT DOES THEIRS?

Special inducements during its introduction elsewhere
Dealers should write for particulars.

UNION SOAP COMPANY, 211 to 221 Arch St.

BALTIMORE.

A mock postmortem with a real cadaver was staged by some local pathologists in 1897, probably at the University of Maryland School of Medicine. (Collection of Ross J. Kelbaugh.)

JOHN W. WEAVER,

(Only Brother to the late John H. Weaver, deceased)

Undertaker of Funerals

IN GENERAL,

No. 129 North Paca Street,

BALTIMORE, MD.

Mechanics and management take a break from work at Goodrich Garage on February 12, 1935. (Collection of Ross J. Kelbaugh.)

A Lexington Market greengrocer works on arranging his display.

Hutzler's department store on Howard Street provided employment for thousands of Baltimoreans from the mid-19th century up to the last quarter of the 20th century. The store, first established in 1858, offered top line clothing and other commodities for city ladies and gents.

This post-World War II photograph shows the choir of Julius Gutman's, another of Baltimore's fine department stores. Mamie Weber sits third from right in the front row. (Courtesy of Ben Weber.)

Nine

COMMERCE AND
RELIGION

"Evergreen" was one the mansions of the Garrett family, a dynasty founded by merchant Robert Garrett, a Scots-Irish immigrant from northern Ireland. In the later 19th century, the Garretts branched into railroads and banking. Their new wealth helped them acquire this classical-style North Charles Street mansion, which was later willed by ambassador John Work Garrett to his alma mater, Johns Hopkins University.

During the Civil War, railroad tycoon John Work Garrett (top) helped run the railways for President Abraham Lincoln. Secretary of War Edwin Stanton praised Garrett's work for the Union cause. In the bottom view, Garrett's railroad, the B&O, is seen as the rail line passes over the strategic Thomas Viaduct west of the city, in one of W. M. Chase's c. 1870 stereo views of "Baltimore and Ohio Railroad Scenery."

The railroad magnate's son, T. Harrison Garrett (top), seemed destined for a long career like his father until he was drowned on Chesapeake Bay in June 1888 when his yacht *Gleam* collided with a Bay ferry near the mouth of the Patapsco. In 1896, his elder son Robert (bottom) won first place medals for the United States in the discus throw and shot put at the first modern Olympic Games in Athens.

Johns Hopkins and Enoch Pratt were two of the city's great benefactors. Hopkins (top), a wealthy Quaker merchant, left a bequest that founded both the Johns Hopkins Hospital (seen here in an early view) and Johns Hopkins University. The generosity of fellow merchant Enoch Pratt (bottom) enabled the founding of the Enoch Pratt Free Library system as well as Sheppard Pratt Hospital. The library's first central branch was on Mulberry Street, shown here.

"Tivoli," the residence of Enoch Pratt, in Govanstown, is seen in the top view, while Johns Hopkins' summer mansion "Clifton," now owned by the City of Baltimore, is seen in the bottom view.

Rev. Jared Sparks (top), later a noted historian and biographer of George Washington, served as first minister of the First Unitarian Church (1818, shown at bottom). The church, at the corner of Charles and Franklin Streets, was designed architect Maximilian Godefroy with decorations by Italian sculptor Antonio Capellano. The pair had earlier collaborated on the city's Battle Monument.

James Cardinal Gibbons was born in Baltimore on July 23, 1834, to Irish immigrant parents. He was appointed a cardinal in 1886. A contemporary wrote that Gibbons was "the simplest of Americans; just the same in the pomp of Rome as in a back street ministering spiritual consolation to a dying negro child." He died on March 24, 1921.

Baltimore has the honor of being the site of the first Catholic cathedral built in the United States. The Basilica of the Assumption, designed by architect Benjamin Henry Latrobe, was completed in 1821 (top). In contrast to the classical design of the Basilica, Mount Vernon Place United Methodist Church (1872, shown at bottom) is strikingly Gothic. A plaque records that it was in a house on this site that Francis Scott Key died while visiting his daughter, Mrs. Charles Howard, in 1843.

A Catholic priest is shown here in an early carte de visite. (Collection of Ann Naito Haney.)

Ben and Ed Weber pose with Rev. Elmer P. Baker of the Church of the Resurrection, Linwood Avenue, Highlandtown. (Courtesy of Ben Weber.)

The Temple of the Baltimore Hebrew Congregation, Madison Avenue, was photographed in the 1890s.

Rev. William Meade Dame, rector of the Memorial Episcopal Church in Bolton Hill, described in his memoirs how he served as a drummer boy in the Confederate Army at Gettysburg.

Ten
FAMILY PORTRAITS

The back of this family portrait is annotated: "1897—Three Generations: Mrs. Margaretta Dorry, died 1906. Nannie Dorry Orem, died 1916. Margaretta Orem."

The boy in this daguerreotype holds a hoop and displays an enchanting Mona Lisa-like smile. The photographer, J. Wistar Davis, worked in Baltimore from 1847 to 1849 out of a studio at the corner of North and Baltimore Streets.

An elderly couple is shown here in a studio photograph with Baltimore's Battle Monument as a backdrop. (Photographs on these two pages from the collection of Ross J. Kelbaugh.)

A young black girl poses for Robert Doyne Darby, who worked out of a studio on N. Gay St. in 1900 to 1901.

A family band is pictured in this portrait by the Baltimore Photographic Company, which worked out of a studio at 588 N. Gay Street during 1896 to 1899. (Both photographs from the collection of Ross J. Kelbaugh.)

This unknown gentleman with a jaunty cravat and with a small smile playing on his lips was photographed at the North Charles Street studio of Blessing & Co., between 1886 through 1904. Perhaps the subject was persuaded to come to the studio by Blessing's reputation for pictures "unsurpassed for brilliancy, beauty, and correctness of effect, and permanency."

A multiple or patented "multigraph" portrait was one of the trick techniques used by the studio photographers. This appealing sequence of photographs of a gentleman in a tophat was taken at the North Charles Street studio of Blessing & Co. (Collection of Ross J. Kelbaugh.)

In the top portrait, an austere looking young lady was captured leaning on a rail fence at the North Charles Street studio of Clinedinst and Son, while in the bottom portrait, Mrs. Charles Morton is the essence of a society belle—all frills and flowers.

On the reverse of this portrait taken at the Baltimore studios of Bachrach and Brothers, Edith Walbridge wrote at Christmas, 1901, "I think my face—like Piper Hamlin's play—will surely serve to scare the rats away."

Pictured in the back yard of 121 Front Street in this c. 1930 view are, from left to right, Lucile Mazula DiPaula, Rosina Mazula, and Margie Mazula Diodati. Just visible at top is the tower of St. Vincent de Paul Church. This entire block of rowhouses was demolished to build the city's new main post office. (Courtesy Elise DiPaula Erlandson and Kathy Lee Erlandson Liston.)

A family dinner with a rabbi was captured by the Hughes Company. (Photography Collections, University of Maryland Baltimore County.)

This African American couple were photographed around 1920 at Lane's Studio at 1631 Pennsylvania Avenue. (Collection of Ross J. Kelbaugh.)

Ellen Beadle and Stephen Komianos are pictured in the front living room of Mrs. Beadle's Park Avenue home. (Courtesy of Dottie Linthicum.)

In this *c.* 1930 Hughes Company photograph, the family makes for a rather charming group, rendered more interesting by the mother's lavish period gown. (Photography Collections, University of Maryland Baltimore County.)

Top: Eliza Linthicum and baby Lowndes Linthicum relax on the front steps of a home on Hawthorne Road, Roland Park. *Bottom:* Mamie Weber with the family dog on the back steps of her Highlandtown home on South Curley Street. (Photographs courtesy of Dottie Linthicum and Ben Weber, respectively.)

Ed and Ben Weber, proud Highlandtown Cub Scouts, are seen here in a snapshot taken in the 1940s. (Courtesy of Ben Weber.)

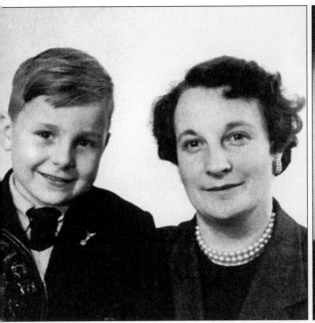

These are the passport photographs of my father and mother, Gordon and Yoria George, and myself. My dad strikes a dashing Ronald Coleman "secret agent" look. We were fresh immigrants to Baltimore from Liverpool, England, in January 1955. I am wearing my dad's Royal Air Force badge. When World War II ended, my father had been demobbed from the RAF, in which he had served in the medical corps as a corporal and physiotherapist (British for "physical therapist"). (Courtesy Yoria C. George.)

This was my mother and myself in 1955 soon after coming to Baltimore from England, experiencing our first American snowfall on Oakford Avenue in Forest Park. (Courtesy Yoria C. George.)

The Weber kids and friends get ready for some fun ice skating. (Courtesy of Ben Weber.)

The photos below are from my family's first Easter Sunday in America (1955). Here we are on Charles Street after the Easter Parade. I already look like a Yank with my new sneakers. The temperature soared to 83 degrees Farenheit! In the lower left photo, Mom and I are standing with the late Edith F. Flavin, with whom we stayed on Guilford Avenue, Charles Village, after our arrival in Baltimore. In the lower right photo, my Dad is holding the inevitable cigarette. He died of cancer in 1979. (Photos courtesy of Yoria C. George.)

Eleven
BEFORE HARBORPLACE

In the decades before the 1980 opening of Harborplace, Baltimore's Inner Harbor wore a very different aspect than it does today. Here we see a view of the Light Street wharves in the 1890s, bustling with commercial activity. A Chesapeake Bay paddle steamer is visible at right. Steamers departed for all destinations round the bay.

These two *c.* 1900 views show traditional bay craft at Baltimore. (Top view, courtesy of the National Archives.)

Both of these views of Baltimore were taken from Federal Hill. *Top:* This view looks north with City Hall at center left and the Shot Tower at right. *Bottom:* The view looking east toward Fells Point and the outer harbor.

Yet another early look at the city from Federal Hill, with coal and lumber yards in the foreground—a c. 1870 stereo view by W. M. Chase. Note the blurred sailing craft, moving too fast for the 10- to 15-second shutter speed. (Collection of Ann Naito Haney.)

Pratt Street is seen here from the water in a pre-Civil War view.

This view of Baltimore was taken as she rebuilt after the disastrous 1904 fire that leveled the city center.

Top: The paddle wheeler *Emma A. Ford* of the Chester River Steamboat Company steams out of the harbor. *Bottom:* This steamship line ad appeared in 1910.

This postcard view of Baltimore from the air around 1940 shows Fort McHenry in the foreground and the city center in the background. The fort was declared a national shrine in 1925. It is visited today by more than 700,000 visitors each year.

This 1940s view of the city skyline was taken looking from the outer harbor.

Pratt Street is seen here looking west *c.* 1900. The traffic unlike today was then two way. Note the traffic congestion with wagons and streetcars clogging the street. Hey! You would almost think the Orioles have a game on down at Camden Yards . . . (Photography Collections, University of Maryland Baltimore County.)